HEY HO LET'S DOUGH

1! 2! 3! 40 Vegan Pizza Recipes Unrelated to the Ramones

Automne Zingg
Recipes by Joshua Ploeg

Microcosm Publishing
Portland, OR

HEY HO LET'S DOUGH
1! 2! 3! 40! Vegan Pizza Recipes Unrelated to the Ramones

Illustrations © 2022 Automne Zingg
Recipes © 2022, Joshua Ploeg
This edition © 2022, Microcosm Publishing
Book design by Joe Biel

First Printing, 7000 copies, May 10, 2022

For a catalog, write
Microcosm Publishing
2752 N. Williams Ave
Portland, OR 97227
or visit Microcosm.Pub/Dough

ISBN 978-1-64841-056-7
This is Microcosm #600

To join the ranks of high-class stores that feature Microcosm titles, talk to your local rep: In the U.S. **COMO** (Atlantic), **FUJII** (Midwest), **BOOK TRAVELERS WEST** (Pacific), **TURNAROUND** (Europe), **UTP/MANDA** (Canada), **NEW SOUTH** (Australia/New Zealand), **GPS** in Asia, Africa, India, South America, and other countries, or **FAIRE** in the gift trade.

Global labor conditions are bad, and our roots in industrial Cleveland in the 70s and 80s made us appreciate the need to treat workers right. Therefore, our books are MADE IN THE USA

Did you know that you can buy our books directly from us at sliding scale rates? Support a small, independent publisher and pay less than Amazon's price at **Microcosm.Pub**

into your pan. Put the leftover dough in a baggie in the fridge or freezer for later and if your roommate tries to steal it shoot 'em in the back. It will keep a week or so in the fridge but you might have to punch it down if it gets too big for the bag. In the freezer it will keep for several months. Preheat oven to 450 degrees. Spread vodka sauce on there. Drizzle some aioli. Do the cheez sauce and cheez next. Then add the "parm," more aioli, and a sprinkle of smoked paprika. Bake for 18-20 minutes or until done to your liking. Tends to generate a good amount of steam so stand back when you take it out.

It is always nice to have a parm mixture like that around, make extra and keep it in the fridge.

MICROCOSM · PUBLISHING

MICROCOSM PUBLISHING is Portland's most diversified publishing house and distributor with a focus on the colorful, authentic, and empowering. Our books and zines have put your power in your hands since 1996, equipping readers to make positive changes in their lives and in the world around them. Microcosm emphasizes skill-building, showing hidden histories, and fostering creativity through challenging conventional publishing wisdom with books and bookettes about DIY skills, food, bicycling, gender, self-care, and social justice. What was once a distro and record label was started by Joe Biel in his bedroom and has become among the oldest independent publishing houses in Portland, OR. We are a politically moderate, centrist publisher in a world that has inched to the right for the past 80 years.

★CONTENTS★

★ CONTENTS ★

PART I: THE BASICS
HEY HO LET'S PIZZA DOUGH

This will be your standard crust here: This makes two pizzas worth of dough… you can store unused dough in the fridge for about a week, or in the freezer for several months. Thaw before use if you've frozen it.

For the Dough

⅔ C. warm water (more or less as needed)

1 envelope dry active yeast

1 tsp. salt (more or less to your taste)

2 Tbsp. olive oil

1 tsp. garlic powder or granulated garlic (optional)

¼ C. cornmeal

2 ½ C. of flour (possibly more), unbleached white is best, or you can make a blend (just make sure it isn't crumbly).

Dissolve yeast in warm water and stir, let sit for 20 minutes to activate. Mix in the rest, adding more flour if needed to make a pliable pizza dough. Knead for a few minutes, then place in a bowl in a warm place, cover loosely with a cloth, and let rise for 45 minutes or more. Punch down, cover again and allow to rise for a couple more hours. You can put it in the fridge overnight if you want to do dough ahead of when you will be using it. When you take it out of the fridge, punch it down and allow it to sit for a bit to get closer to room temperature, which takes 30 minutes to an hour. You're going through a tight wind and don't want any curveballs.

You can speed up yeast activation with a little sugar, but it is not necessary—I have been yelled at by people from Italy for both using and not using sugar. Meanwhile just do whatever people in Connecticut do, since they seem to know what they are talking about.

Roll half of your dough out on a floured board, you can also use your hands, toss, whatever you like. For the last part of rolling and/or pulling, dust it with a bit of cornmeal and fit it to your pan. A 14" pizza pan is suitable for an ideal crust, you can use a smaller pan but that will make for a thicker crust. If you love thick crusts, well then you go ahead. Alternatively, let it rise in the pan a bit before baking, just be aware it might not rise evenly and you may have to compensate. Obviously you can use a little less dough for a thinner crust or roll it out as thin as you want and cut the edge off. Generally, I like to liberally grease the pan and dust with cornmeal, and bake at 450°. You can go higher or lower, just know that this obviously will make it take more cooking time or less, and the positioning of your racks matters. You will need to make adjustments accordingly on both fronts. I bake one rung above the middle usually, but use your best judgment. Every oven is different and it may be a good idea to use an oven thermometer in order to know if your oven runs hot or cold. With vegan pizzas some cheezes just don't exactly...melt, so trial and error with various brands or combinations will get you where you want to be.

Not wanting to stop there, let's make this an actual pizza:

Hemp Heart Parm

Mix:

½ C. hulled hemp seeds

1 Tbsp. toasted crushed sesame seeds

2 Tbsp. nutritional yeast

1 tsp. garlic powder

Salt and pepper to taste (kind of a lot of salt, use half truffle salt)

Aioli

Blend:

6 smashed, peeled garlic cloves

½ to 1 tsp. salt depending on your taste

¼ C. olive oil

1 Tbsp. lemon juice

When blending, start with garlic, salt, lemon juice, then slowly add oil.

½ C. spicy cheez sauce (use any cheez sauce recipe in this book or your favorite recipe but add roasted spicy chilies or chili sauce to taste)

1 C. grated vegan cheez, or 12 discs made from slices of white cheez

Chili vodka sauce- you want 1 ½ C. pizza sauce or marinara with ¼ C. vodka, ¼ C. vegan milk and 2 roasted fresno or serrano chilies, blended together for your sauce, then heat that in a saucepan til bubbling and turn off heat after 5 minutes.

Sprinkle with smoked paprika

The kind of pizza you eat before or after a show, a little heat, a little drinky… Prepare pizza dough as above and get one pizza's worth of it

★NOW I WANNA SNIFF CASHEWS

Cashew Cheez

This is also your general cheezy sauce.

Soak 1 C. raw cashews in water overnight

Drain water and then blend until smooth with:

⅔ C. unsweetened cashew milk (use more as needed)

2 Tbsp. truffle oil

1 Tbsp. cider vinegar

1 Tbsp. prepared Dijon mustard

2 peeled, smashed garlic cloves

½ to 1 tsp. ground turmeric or asafoetida (dealer's choice)

Smoky salt to taste

You can add nooch also if you want, it's not necessary

Cashew Crust (very expensive)

1 pkg. yeast

1 C. warm water

Activate yeast in warm water until it bubbles

Meanwhile, grind:

2 C. cashews into a meal

Mix in:

1 Tbsp. xanthan gum

⅓ C. tapioca flour

⅓ C. quinoa flour

⅓ C. brown rice flour or sorghum flour

salt to taste

Make a well and add:

yeast mixture and

2 Tbsp. olive oil

Mix well in a bowl and then place covered in a warm spot for a couple of hours.

You'll also need:

2 C. pizza sauce (see EXTRA! recipe pg. 24)

1 C. roasted cashews

A dozen or so halved pickled cherry peppers

2 Tbsp. minced fresh herbs

½ C. thinly sliced red onion

I put a lot of instructions in the ingredients list, well if you haven't blown your brain out sniffing glue you should be able to follow it, whereas I have and can't! Hahahaha — sufferrrrr!!

1-2-3-4-

Line a pizza pan with parchment and press the crust evenly in there. Bake at 350 degrees for 15 minutes. Take it out of the oven and spread pizza sauce on there, add red onions, roasted cashews, and cherry peppers, drizzle with cheezy sauce and sprinkle with herbs.

Bake for another 15 minutes or so, until it looks good. You can hit the top with the broiler to get it right if you must. These GF crusts tend to dry out and this one might be a bit more of a forker than a hand-held deal.

If you really want, you can replace the almonds in the sausage in Beet on the Brat (pg. 72) with cashews and put that on here as well. All the kids are doing it.

Probably any one of these cashew components on a pizza is okay, all of them is likely questionable. Could be like 6,000 calories a slice if you're paranoid and keep track of that sort of thing.

★ GENERALLY A SHREDDABLE CHEEZ, WITH VARIATIONS

1 C. raw cashews (use sesame seeds for tahini cheez, hulled is best)

1 C. favorite unsweetened vegan milk, such as oat

1 ½ Tbsp. agar powder

⅓ C. tapioca starch

2 Tbsp. olive oil

2 Tbsp. truffle oil

1 Tbsp. nutritional yeast

1 Tbsp. prepared horseradish or tasty mustard

1 Tbsp. lemon juice or white wine vinegar, more would be good for tahini cheez

1 tsp. of salt, more to taste of course and personally I like smoky salt as part of this

If doing tahini cheez, add 2 chopped garlic cloves to the blender

Soak cashews or sesame seeds in enough water to cover them and leave them overnight, rinse and drain. Puree with vegan milk, mustard, nutritional yeast, tapioca starch, and olive oil until smooth. Heat in a saucepan over medium-low. As it begins to heat up, whisk in agar, salt, and truffle oil. Once it begins to thicken (after a few minutes), stir in vinegar and remove from heat. Allow it to cool a bit then remove from pan and mold it into your desired shape, wrap tightly in plastic wrap or parchment or place into a mold and cover, and keep it in the fridge overnight. It will be a bit soft and possibly sticky or spongy at first but should stiffen up enough to slice or even grate after a sit in the fridge. You can mold it in a large ramekin or bowl for a disk or dome shape, or form it into a ball if you are at a loss for how to form it. The agar will give it a slight amount of meltiness and you should be able to shred or grate it at least somewhat. Play around with different flavorings and amounts of thickener and such for more interesting variations. Hard to get cheezes just right, bullshit scum they disintegrate!

You could use almonds, macadamia nuts, or combinations of different nuts for this as well.

Don't want to use nuts? Then cooked mashed potatoes or white beans do the trick, most likely requiring a bit more thickener of one sort or another.

Should smell a bit like a wet warthog.

★COMMANDOUGH

1-2-3-4…first rule is…

4 C. flour

2 C. water

1 pkg. dry active yeast

kosher salt to taste

cornmeal

etc.

For the Filling

1 C. grated cheez

1 C. marinara (see Go Little Marinara pg. 65)

½ C. chopped olives

1 C. chopped squash blossoms, sauteed with onion, garlic, and salt and
  pepper

½ C. diced red onion

1 C. chopped roasted pepper

½ C. cooked seasoned black beans

olive oil for various purposes

We're going to dough along with Automne's basic concept on this one, except keeping in the realm of commandos we're going to take it more into "Lawyers, Guns & Money" or "If I Had a Rocket Launcher" type of territory, instead of just sticking around Berlin and old Hanoi. So, a fried (or grilled) dough pocket is in order. I would explain this more but I don't talk to commies.

Activate yeast in warm water, then add flour and salt and a handful of cornmeal at this point. Make a workable dough and knead until smooth, then coat lightly in oil, place in a bowl and cover with a light cloth, and allow to rise in a warm place for a couple of hours. Punch down.

Once the dough is risen and punched down, you're going to want to use the cornmeal to make it stiff enough to handle without getting too sticky or puffing up wayyyy too much in the fryer, according to the laws of Germany

So, divide the dough into 16 balls, using cornmeal to coat your surface for rolling, you want these to be about ¼" thick. I would roll them out in pairs, you're going to make 8 of these buggers. To make one, take one dough round and place a generous dollop of whatever filling or combo thereof out of those listed above that you want to use. Place another round on top of this and use your fingers to punch down a seal around the filling, then seal the edge thoroughly all the way around and set aside. Once you have all of them ready to go, you can either bake at 425 degrees on greased baking pans, making sure to brush the tops with olive oil, for about 20 minutes... or you can do a shallow pan fry (just coat the pan in oil or use less than ¼" depth of oil in there), in batches, turning once, until browned on both sides. Or if you are risky and have a little clapper thing that will hold it together you can deep fry them at 350 until browned. In this case you really want to make sure your seal is really sealed. I would also recommend making smaller ones in this case. You can do this by folding one round of dough over and sealing it like an empanada. Anyway, have fun with this one.

★EXTRA! AN EASY PIZZA SAUCE!

Puree

2 C. stewed tomatoes

¼ C. broth or tomato juice

2 Tbsp. tomato paste

¼ C. olive oil

Salt and pepper to taste

1 Tbsp. balsamic vinegar

¼ tsp. red pepper flakes (more for hotter)

1 tsp. onion powder

1 ½ tsp. garlic powder

2 tsp. dried Italian herbs

Let it sit to flavor up before using, keeps in the fridge for a week or two... thinner? thicker? add more broth or some tomato juice for thinner, add more tomato paste for thicker. Want to make from scratch? Haha- well you can easily stew tomatoes yourself, act like you are going to make the marinara in this book to do that. You'll have to look up a tomato paste recipe, you won't be finding one here! Just get your hammer and smash that smash that tomato.

★IMITATION WHEAT GERM FOR GLUTEN FREE WEIRDOS

Use 1 C. golden flax meal

1 Tbsp. nutritional yeast

smoked salt or interesting
   seasoned salt to taste

1 Tbsp. dried Italian herbs

2 tsp. granulated garlic

¼ C. toasted ground hazelnuts

Put this on everything. Don't worry we are all weirdos I'm not making fun of you. That's in the past and history is not where I wanna be.

★TO MAKE A WHITE SAUCE A CHEEZY SAUCE

If all those damn cashews are too expensive, add half a cup of grated cheez to the white sauce from Here Today... (Pg. 111), should work out great!

★ CONVERT IT

There are a few different crust and sauce recipes in here, sometimes you get referred in one recipe to another, it happens. You can mix and match however you like just be aware of how that might change cooking times, order, and taste.

It is up to you if you prefer one commercial cheez or another, to use one of my cheezes or white sauces or your own. Some melt, some do not. We're not here to hold your hand through this process, so I'm sure you can figure it out and quit your whining.

I heard a rumour people wanted more complicated recipes this time, I don't care! Be careful what you wish for.

Bon crapetit!

Cup	Fluid OZ	TBSP	TSP	Milliliter
1 C	8 oz	16 Tbsp	48 tsp	237 ml
3/4 C	6 oz	12 Tbsp	36 tsp	177 ml
2/3 C	5 1/3 oz	10.6 Tbsp	32 tsp	158 ml
1/2 C	4 oz	8 Tbsp	24 tsp	118 ml
1/3 C	2 2/3 oz	5.3 Tbsp	16 tsp	79 ml
1/4 C	2 oz	4 Tbsp	12 tsp	59 ml
1/8 C	1 oz	2 Tbsp	6 tsp	30 ml
1/16 C	1/2 oz	1 Tbsp	3 tsp	15 ml

PART II: THE RECIPES

★ CALIFORNIA SUNDRIED TOMATO

You will need...

Pizza dough for 1 pizza

Sundried Tomato Sauce

1 ½ C. pizza sauce

½ C. sundried tomatoes

1 Tbsp. white balsamic

a pinch each of oregano, sea salt, black pepper, garlic powder

^ puree that

½ C. diced red onion

½ C. chopped olives

½ C. smoky sundried tomatoes, julienne

¼ C. basil leaves cut into thin strips

1 C. grated cheez or cheezy sauce

red pepper flakes

capers

Prepare dough as stated a million times and get it in the damn pan!

Saute red onions in olive oil and a little salt and pepper until soft. Puree pizza sauce and extras together. Spread sauce on pizza crust, then olives, red onions, and sundried tomatoes and basil, then cheez, capers, and pepper flakes—are we out here having fun yet?

Well that's good because now it's time to bake at 450 degrees for about 20 minutes, a little longer if necessary, a little less if unnecessary—the patience is short but the minutes are long, take my word for it.

★TEXAS CHAIN SAUCE MASSACRE

Pizza dough for 1 pizza

Olive oil

2 C. grated cheez or cheez sauce

1 C. chopped veggie sausage

½ C. sliced black olives

1 C. diced tomatoes

1 C. diced onion

½ C. diced green bell peppers

Salt and pepper

3 C. pizza sauce (see EXTRA! recipe pg. 24)

1 Tbsp. minced fresh oregano

Prepare pizza dough or else you'll never get out of there, and—

For this use a large cast iron pan, grease quite liberally with olive oil. Roll crust out to fit, going up the sides a bit and press it into the pan. Sprinkle with cheez, then top with sausage, olives, green peppers, onions, and tomatoes. Sprinkle with salt and pepper, pour 2 C. sauce over this and sprinkle with oregano. Bake at 425 degrees for half an hour to 40 minutes, or until it looks pretty good. Allow to cool down for a few minutes, then cut and serve with more pizza sauce warmed up and poured onto the plate.

If you want to cut it with a chainsaw when you serve I say go ahead… actually it would be best to turn the whole thing out upside down on a platter, dump the extra sauce all over it, and then cut it up with one of those electric turkey slicers while wearing a mask.

Just my two cents.

★ CARBONARA NOT GLUE

Pizza dough for 1 pizza

Penne to make 2 C. cooked

"Cream" Sauce

½ c. raw cashews, soaked overnight and drained

½ C. cooked mashed potato or ⅓ C. potato starch

¼ tsp. smoked salt

1 Tbsp. truffle oil

1 ½ C. kreem

2 Tbsp. margarine

2 minced or pressed peeled garlic cloves

1 tsp. lemon juice

1 Tbsp. ground hemp seed or nutritional yeast

Blend all of this^ to make a creamy sauce.

Some olive oil for saute

1 C. chopped veggie bacon

1 minced garlic clove

Freshly cracked black pepper

¼ C. chopped onion

Chopped scallion

1 C. white sauce (Here Today… Pg. 110) or pizza sauce (see EXTRA! recipe pg. 24)

1 C. grated vegan cheez

Roach Spray Recipe

Chop a head of garlic, skin and all and simmer it in 1 C. olive oil or other favorite oil for 2-3 minutes, use a heavy pot that is larger than seems necessary, just to be on the safe side. Turn off heat and add a sprig of chopped oregano, 2 tsp. chili flakes, and 1 tsp. salt. Cool and then pour all in a container with a lid. Let sit 24 hours, shaking occasionally. Strain and put in an oil spraying bottle, you can also drizzle instead for use if you don't have a spray bottle suitable for oil.

Prepare yo dough. Get it in the greased pan.

Boil and drain pasta, pretty al dente.

While that's happening, fry bacon,onion, and garlic in a pan coated in olive oil with some salt and black pepper.

Heat sauce in a pot and cook for 5 minutes, add pasta to coat and incorporate thoroughly. Add bacon, scallions, and black pepper to taste and roach spray too and set aside.

Spread pizza sauce or white sauce on pizza, then penne mixture, then cheez and bake at 450 degrees for about 22 minutes.

Pasta on pizza is pretty wuvvable.

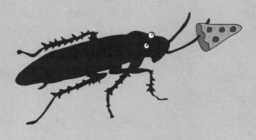

★I TOOK THE CRUST AND THREW IT AWAY

For the Pumpkin Marinara

1 C. marinara sauce (see Go Little Marinara pg. 65)

1 C. roasted or canned pumpkin, mashed (butternut squash also works)

Salt and pepper

2 Tbsp. olive oil

¼ C. red wine

For the Pumpkin Dumplings

1 C. rice flour

1 C. cornmeal

¼ C. tapioca flour

1 ½ tsp. baking powder

¾ C. quinoa flour or millet flour

1 pkg. dry yeast

1 Tbsp. sugar

1 tsp. Salt

1 C. roasted or canned pumpkin

1 ½ tsp. curry powder

2 Tbsp. olive oil

⅓ C. warm broth or water, more as needed to make dough

1 C. thinly sliced red onions

1 C. arugula leaves

1 C. shredded cheez or cheez sauce

1 C. halved cherry tomatoes

Salt, pepper, and olive oil to taste

This is a bit of a deconstructed pizza, I can't miss out on anything trendy, even if that trend is a bit passé. The dumplings take the place of the crust in a way, and some pizzas out there are even cooked upside down, so I don't feel bad about this one!

Mix together yeast, sugar, and ⅓ C. warm water and let stand for 10 minutes. Mix in other wet ingredients, then mix dry together separately and add them to make a soft dough. Use more liquid or flour as needed, it should be soft but not overly sticky, this could make a never ending supply. Allow to sit covered in a warm place for several hours.

Make the pumpkin marinara by mixing the ingredients in that section together. Set aside.

Now bring a large pot of lightly salted water to a boil. Form dough into dumplings and drop them in, boiling for about 15 minutes. Drain and set aside.

Turn on your broiler and grease a large cast iron skillet or a casserole dish. Place dumplings in here, then pumpkin sauce on top. Next cheez and toppings, except for the arugula. Shalalala sprinkle with salt and pepper and broil for 5-7 minutes or until cheez melts and there is some grilly looking stuff going on. When it's ready, take it out and scatter the arugula on top then drizzle with a little olive oil. A nice balsamic drizzle or truffle oil and a smatter of red pepper flakes are also great. As is sriracha or a similar sauce, heat it up until it's sparking in the night awooo!

Deconstructed anything remains popular to this day, I think fad food tends to go in waves, with it getting rediscovered where it first started by the time everyone has gotten around to hearing about it, so what 22 years?

I once read that the original pizza-like substance was something like a dumpling soaked in sauce or vinegar that soldiers kept under their helmet so this is, like, keeping with tradition rather than fucking with it.

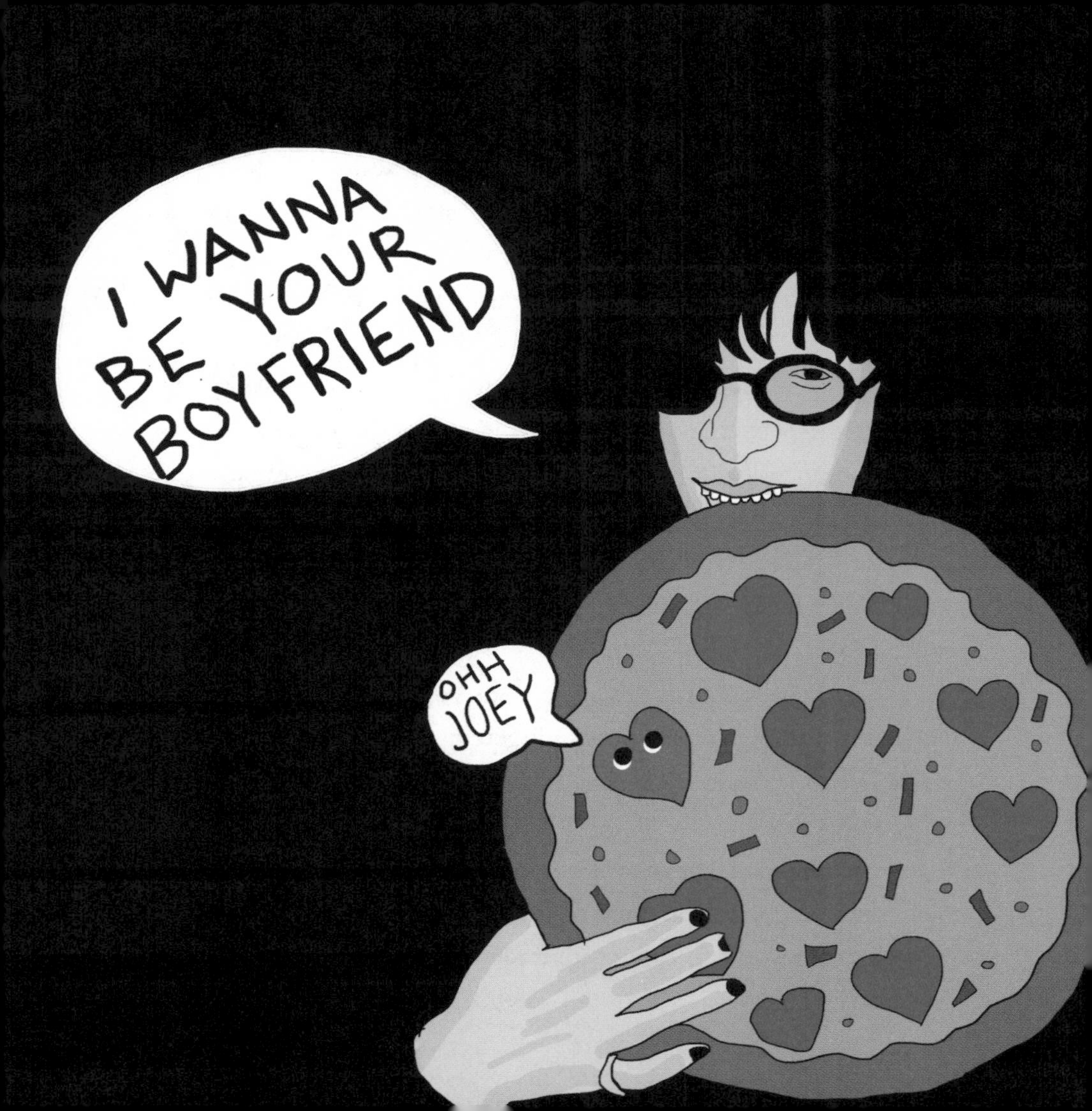
I WANNA BE YOUR BOYFRIEND
OHH JOEY

★I WANNA BE YOUR BOYFRIEND

Pizza dough for 1 pizza

1 C. pizza sauce + a roasted bell pepper blended in

1 C. tomatillo sauce with a roasted serrano pepper or two. Also works well with a pesto (see Poison Artichoke Heart pg. 61 or 1-2-3-4 pg. 69)

12 basil leaves

½ C. diced onion

2 minced garlic cloves

Olive oil

½ C. pine nuts or walnuts

16 slices veggie pepperoni

½ C. sliced green olives

½ C. sliced black

1 C. grated cheez or cheez sauce

Salt and pepper

Because relationships are such troubles I was thinking something like pizza divorciado, even you can have this relationship in your head and then on this pizza and then never actually have to go out with the person. *"So what happened?!"... "Oh it didn't work out... I ate a pizza and thought about it!"* Anyway this is a sweet little pizza here.

Prepare pizza dough as always and get it into a greased pan. Cover one half with red sauce, one half with green. Sprinkle with onions and garlic and then cheez. Next let's mix it up and actually put the nuts, basil leaves, and green olives on the red half, and then the pepperoni and black olives on the green half. Drizzle with a little olive oil and sprinkle with salt and pepper and bake at 450 degrees for 18-20 minutes, or until done in your hot little oven.

Wanting to be, becoming and unbecoming are all a fun part of the process. Not sad at all!

What can I say?!

★PIZZA THERAPY

That might not be all they wanna give me but it's all that I want...

1 C. sauteed mushrooms

½ C. chopped red onion

½ C. chopped white onion

½ C. chopped scallion

⅔ C. pizza sauce (see EXTRA! recipe pg. 24)

⅔ C. white sauce (see Here Today... pg. 110)

⅔ C. either one of the green sauces or white sauce mixed with red and a little beet juice or beet pureed in (for green sauces see Poison Artichoke Heart pg. 59 or 1-2-3-4 pg. 69)

½ C. grated white cheez (this means any old shredded or grateable cheez that is white, in case you haven't figured that out by now)

Pizza dough for 1 pizza

Prepare the crust and get it into a greased pan. Make a fun spiral pattern with the three sauces. Very important. Sprinkle the white area with white onion and cheez, the green or pink/purple area with scallions and the red area with red onion. Scatter mushrooms over it all and bake at 450 degrees for about 20 minutes.

There are a lot of variations you could do on this obviously, such as using the chioga beet bacon, making a green or red coloured cheez, etc., keeps it edgy and mean. Imagination is key for psychoactive therapy.

If you didn't have problems before, you will after this.

What happens if you use psychedelic mushrooms on here? Probably something really good however don't keep them around someone may burglarize your home… and then still be there when you get back lying on the floor in a swirl of sauces going "my pizza is just right."

TWENTY TWENTY TWENTY TWENTY FOUR HOURS TO GO OHH OHH
I WANNA BE SAUTÉED
KISS THE COOK

★I WANNA BE SAUTEED

1 C. chopped veggie turkee

12 halved brussels sprouts

½ C. diced white onion

1 C. diced sweet potato

6 vegan marshmallows cut in half

Olive oil for saute

½ C. cranberry sauce

1 C. gravy (see KKK recipe pg. 123… now there's some fun optics)

1 C. pizza sauce (see EXTRA! recipe pg. 24)

1 C. grated vegan cheez

Pizza dough for 1 pizza

Sauteed Stuffing

1 C. bread or cornbread, cubed

¼ C. chopped onion

¼ C. chopped celery

¼ C. chopped water chestnuts

1 tsp. minced fresh sage

½ tsp. minced fresh rosemary

½ C. broth

Salt and pepper to taste

¼ C. margarine or olive oil

2 Tbsp. soy sauce

Get it? Because Thanksgiving food… oh never mind.

Probably got too much going on here but the boys from Queens were nothing if not complicated.

Let's see, stuffing first: start by melting margarine (or use oil) in a pan, then add the listed vegetables and saute for 2 minutes. Then the herbs and bread and saute that for 2 minutes, then the seasonings and broth… cook for a couple more minutes or until the broth is absorbed, set aside.

Saute the brussels next in a little oil with some salt and

pepper, after 3-4 minutes, add onion, cook for several minutes more, then add your turkee and cook until browned a bit. Set aside.

Next cook sweet potatoes in a little oil for a few minutes, deglaze with a little water or broth after about 5 minutes, season and cook until sweet potatoes are of an edible texture. Place marshmallow pieces atop and broil in the oven until they get a little scorch, will not take very long. Or use a torch if you can control your fingers. Set aside.

Prepare the ol' pizza dough and get it in the pan. Pizza sauce and gravy go on next, then stuffing, then dollop with cranberry sauce here and there, then do the cheez or change the order if you can control your brain… array the turkee/brussels mix next and get it in the oven before you go insane. Bake at 450 degrees for 15 minutes, then hurry hurry and array the sweet potatoes/marshmallows concoction atop and cook for another 5 minutes or so.

★YOU SHOULD HAVE NEVER OPENED THAT DOOR

Ooooh… scarrry!!

1 C. pizza sauce with ¼ C. roasted or pickled beets blended in (see EXTRA! recipe pg. 24)

1 C. cheezy sauce with 1 tsp. charcoal powder added (for a cheezy sauce see Now I Wanna Sniff Cashews pg. 15)

1 C. purple corn/black corn kernels, roasted or sauteed

1 C. chopped red cabbage, sauteed and seasoned with salt, pepper, and dill

½ C. chopped assorted pickles, the weirder the better

¼ C. balsamic glaze

½ C. grated cheez

½ C. grated or crumbled tahini cheez using black sesame (see tahini variation on shreddable cheez recipe pg. 18)

Pizza dough for 1 pizza with a tablespoon or so of charcoal powder added

Seaweed, I recommend using reconstituted hijiki (it looks like little bats!)

More ominous to your intestines and back end than it even looks to the eyes! Set your dough right here on the altar and prepare this pizza dough as you normally would but mix in the charcoal powder to blacken the dough. If I were you I would roll this out on a plastic-wrap covered board or a big flexi board to avoid getting that charcoal on a wooden board or counter top, but you know, live dangerously.

Alternate the pizza sauce and the cheezy sauce in some interesting pattern. Do the cabbage next, then sprinkle the two grated cheezes on, then decorate with the corn and pickles, seaweed if you are using it, and bake at 450 degrees for 18-20 minutes or until satisfactory.

What you can do with this axe is chop it up.

★I WANT YOU AROUND

24 veggie pepperoni or salami slices, cut into hearts

Green olive tapenade, mix

½ C. chopped green olives

¼ C. chopped red onions

1 tsp. minced rosemary and marjoram

2 tsp. olive oil

1 tsp. red wine vinegar

Salt and pepper to taste

Pink Love Sauce:

Mix 1 ⅓ C. pizza sauce with ⅔ C. white sauce (see EXTRA! recipe pg. 24 for pizza sauce and Here Today... Pg. 110, respectively)

1 C. artichoke hearts, chopped

Pizza dough for 1 pizza

1 C. grated cheez

I'm sure you can figure out how to cut pepperonis and salamis into heart shapes. What to do with the bits? Well, you can make a miniature antipasti or maybe stick them in the Commandough pocket, or use them to make a more interesting meatball.

Prepare pizza crust and get it into a pan. Do not kiss the dough, but feel the dough. It may try to resist but just try to make things clear and it should be an ordinary day. Heat oven to 450 degrees. Spread pink sauce on it, then artichoke hearts and tapenade, then sprinkle with cheez, then decorate with hearts and bake for about 20 minutes.

Just listen to Innervisions on replay.

★I JUST WANNA HAVE SOMETHING TO DOUGH

1 ½ C. chopped veggie chickn

⅔ C. pizza sauce (see EXTRA! recipe pg. 24)

1 C. diced potato

½ C. chopped white onion

1 ½ C. grated vegan cheez

Pizza dough for 1 pizza but add 2 tsp. curry powder to dough or brush with curry oil once in the pan

For the Vindaloo Sauce

2 Tbsp. vinegar

2 Tbsp. brown sugar

2 tsp. Turmeric

¼ C. minced onion

2 dried chilies

2 peeled, smashed garlic cloves

2 tsp. chopped ginger

1 tsp. cumin seed

1 tsp. coriander seeds

¼ C. chopped cilantro

1 black mustard seed

1 Tbsp. garam masala

1" cinnamon stick, cracked

½ tsp. black peppercorns

2 Tbsp. tamarind paste

1 Tbsp. tomato paste

2 Tbsp. olive oil

1 C. broth

Striving here to make this vindaloo different from those of past cookbooks.

Prepare your dough all by yourself and get it in the pan.

Make your vindaloo sauce by toasting spices, garlic, and onion in a dry pan for a minute or two, basically until you can smell them, add oil, salt and pepper to taste, and pastes… stir in broth and simmer for a couple of minutes. Adjust seasonings and set aside to cool down. Once it is not super hot, puree it into a nice sauce. Reminisce about the smells of 2nd Avenue.

Start frying potatoes in a little oil, add salt and pepper… as they start to brown add onions and chickn… season that with a little spice and such if you want… when it's done, toss with some of your vindaloo sauce.

Spread remaining vindaloo sauce mixed with pizza sauce over your pizza. Sprinkle with half of the cheez, array chickn and potato mixture on there, followed by the rest of the cheez and bake at 450 degrees for about 20 minutes. You know you don't want to share this with anybody else.

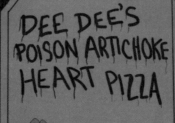

★POISON ARTICHOKE HEART

8 eggplant slices, ½" thick, sauteed in some olive oil with salt and pepper until a little soft

½ C. grated potato, fried until crispy with salt and pepper

1 thinly sliced tomato, dredged in cornmeal and chili powder, salt and pepper

For the Tomatillo Sauce

1 C. peeled and chopped tomatillos

½ C. chopped white onion

2 peeled smashed garlic cloves

1 bay leaf

Salt

1 Tbsp. olive oil

1 tsp. dried oregano

¼ C. mushroom broth

½ C. chopped artichoke hearts

½ C. sliced artichoke hearts, coated in seasoned cornmeal and fried until crispy

Pizza dough for 1 pizza

1 C. grated cheez

These toppings were all either once poisonous before cultivation or people thought they were. In case you didn't know! To this day there are still weirdos that won't eat this stuff (no offence weirdos!).

Roast tomatillos, onion, garlic, and bay leaf with a little salt and olive oil to coat at 375 degrees for 25 minutes. Allow to cool for a bit and then puree with broth, add more broth if you need to.

You can leave the bay leaf in for a puree, since it will get chopped up. The whole spine is what can poke you, which is why people tend to take it out when using a whole one in sauces. If your blender is weak, take it out.

Prepare pizza dough and get it into the pan, slather with tomatillo sauce, place eggplant, chopped artichoke hearts, tomato slices, and cheez on top, then sprinkle with fried potatoes and crispy artichoke and bake at 450 degrees for 20-22 minutes. It might take less time, whatever, you'll figure it out, don't be a drumbeat behind, helpless child.

You'll notice there were a lot of actions included in the ingredients list, yeah I do that a lot, sorry if it really shakes you up.

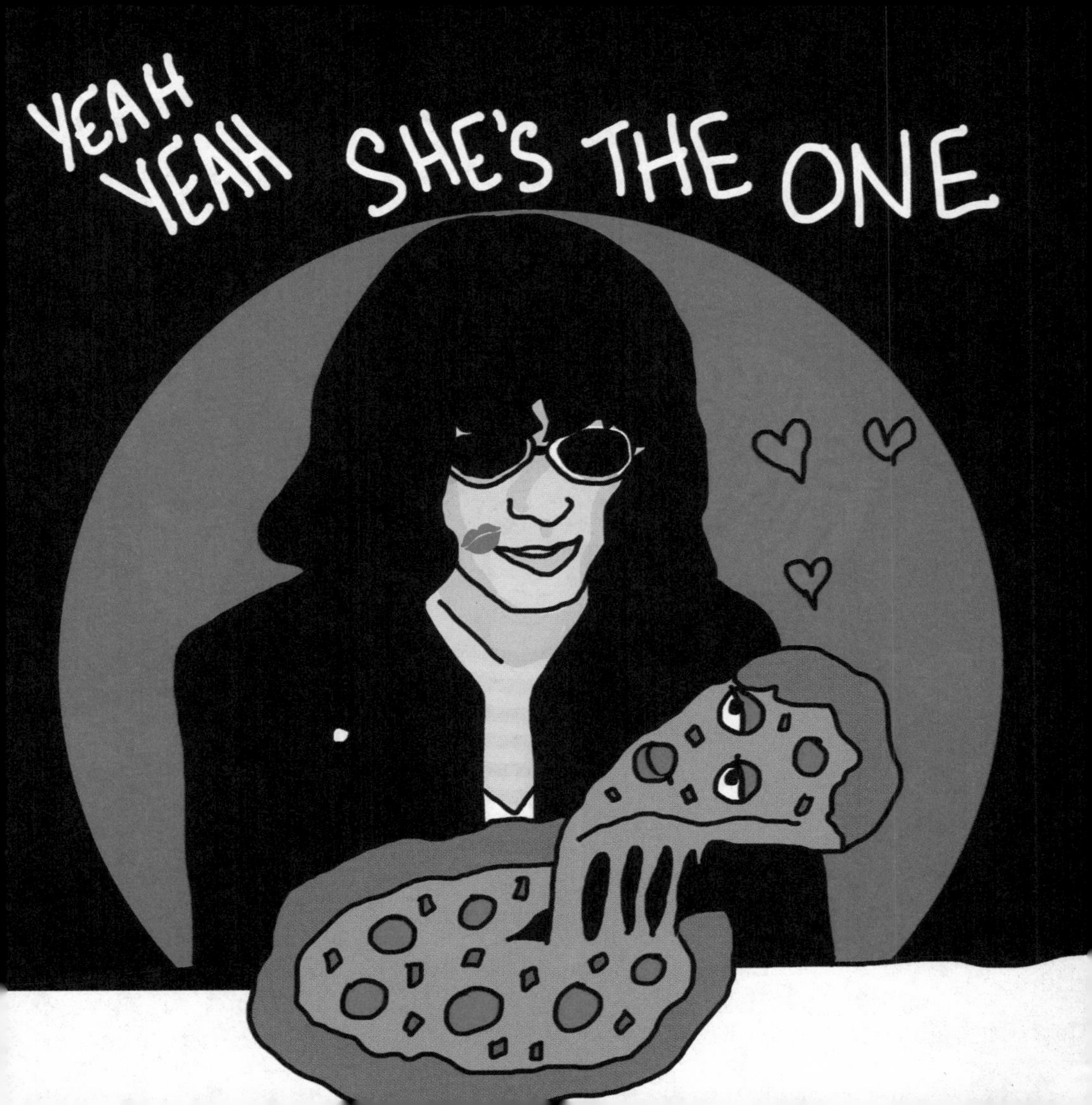
YEAH YEAH SHE'S THE ONE

★GO LITTLE MARINARA GO

3 lbs. tomatoes, first of all you're going to want to use Roma or a similar Italian variety

¼ C. olive oil

1 Tbsp. fresh oregano leaves

4 or 5 fresh chopped basil leaves

5 smashed, peeled garlic cloves

½ C. diced onion

¼ C. grated carrot

½ tsp. chili flake

⅓ C. red wine

1 bay leaf

Salt and pepper to taste

1 to 2 C. broth or tomato juice, more or less as needed

Pizza dough for 1 pizza

Basil leaves

12 rounds of sliced cheez

Pizza marinara is the sort of thing you make when you are extra proud of your tomatoes, or if you don't have anything else to put on it.

Peel your tomatoes (you can either try to get the peel off deftly with your fingernails or steam them for two minutes and THEN peel, in which case be careful as they will be hot), then place in a pot with a drizzle of the oil, some salt and pepper, bay leaf, garlic, onion, and begin to saute. After a couple of minutes add half a cup of your broth and cover. Lower heat and cook for 20 minutes, then remove the lid and add the rest of the ingredients, keeping an eye on how much liquid you need for the thickness you want. Give everything a smash with a potato masher or other thing, simmer for about 5 minutes, then smash again. It's fun. Good times for everyone! Simmer for another 10 minutes or so, still keeping an eye on how watery it seems, then go at it with an immersion blender to make a smoother texture. Adjust seasoning to taste, allow to cool for a little while, then put it in jars and place in the fridge until further use.

Get your dough ready and into the pan.

Shake baby shake the marinara in the jar-ah. Spread the required amount on the pizza. Then place cheez strategically, then basil leaves.

Easy to leave the cheez off, it doesn't have cheez! It never has cheez!

Bake at 450 degrees for about 18 minutes.

★1-2-3-4 PIZZA QUATTRO

1-2-3-4

Hmmm. . . what four sauces should we go for?

Pesto, marinara, white sauce, and how about a yellow squash?

About ¾ C *pesto*

Blend ¼ C. olive oil, ¼ C. pine nuts or walnuts, 1 tsp. lemon juice or white wine vinegar, salt to taste, ¼ C. chopped basil, and 1 Tbsp. of that hemp seed parm

Yellow Squash Sauce

Saute ½ C. chopped yellow squash and blend with 2 Tbsp. olive oil, ¼ C. broth, ¼ C. diced onion, salt and pepper to taste, 1 tsp. fresh thyme leaves, 1 Tbsp. yellow corn meal, 1 Tbsp. lemon juice, 2 peeled smashed garlic cloves, and a couple of saffron threads

1-2-3-4-

You'll also need ½ to ¾ C. *white sauce*

½ C. to ¾ C. *pizza sauce or marinara*

2 C. grated cheezes or cheez sauces, try doing 4 different ones in ½ C. each, mix and match however you like

I don't really think this pizza requires any more toppings than these sauces and cheezes to be honest

This time I want you to have a 16" pan at least, 18" is great if you have it. Get the dough prepared and into this fabulous pan. Score this beauty into 4 equal "slices." Don't slice through though, just mark the dough.

1-2-3-4-

Obviously what you do next is spread each sauce on its own quarter. Be your own judge about how much is enough, using all of the sauce is a fair amount, you might prefer less. Next do all of your fabulous cheezes. Bake at 450 degrees of course for around 20 minutes or until done to your liking.

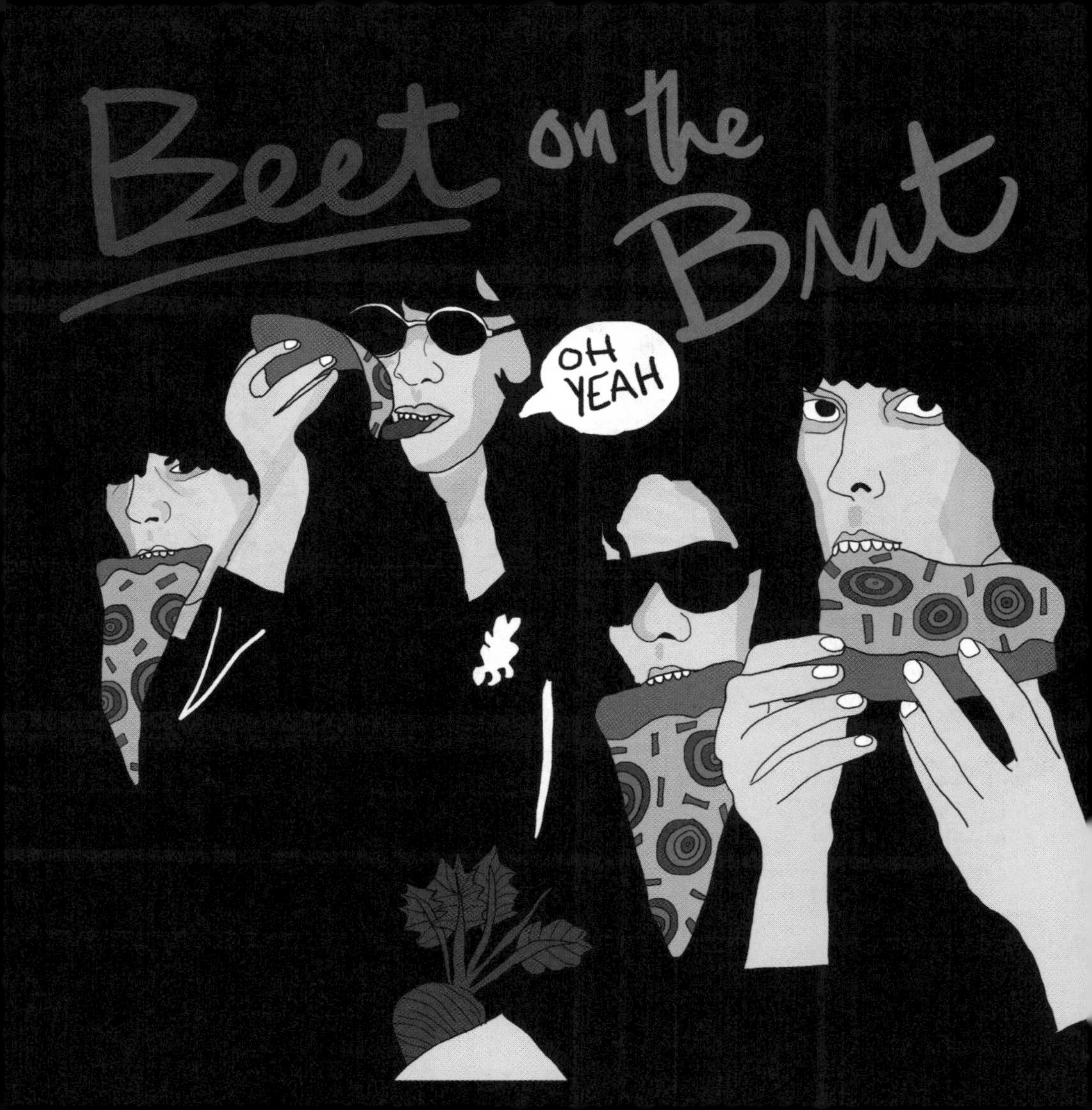
Beet on the Brat
OH YEAH

★BEET ON THE BRAT

24 chioggia beet rounds sliced ⅛" thick

Seasoning mix: 1 tsp. smoked paprika, ½ tsp. smoked salt, 2 Tbsp. tamari or favorite aminos, ½ tsp. black pepper, 1 tsp. cider vinegar or other tangy substance, 2 Tbsp. olive oil or other favorite oil

Sausages (your favorite sort of brat, sliced or see recipe below)

½ C. sliced black olives

Pizza dough for 1 pizza

2 C. pizza sauce (see EXTRA! recipe pg. 24) add a little beet juice

1 tsp. garlic powder

1 C. grated vegan cheez or cheez sauce

Next of all I would peel the beets and slice them thinly, oh yeah. Although it's also fine to leave the peel on, oh yeah. And then set them in a single layer on paper towels and salt them lightly, oh yeah. After 10 minutes pat them dry and toss in the seasoning mix, oh-oh.

That is too many oh yeahs. But you'll live.

Place them (the beet rounds, not the oh yeahs) in a single layer on a parchment-lined baking sheet and bake at 400 degrees for 10 minutes, flip them over and bake for another 10-15 minutes or until they seem a bit crispy. Set aside. You might as well leave the oven on, raise the temperature now to 450 degrees.

Lightly grease a 14"-16" pizza pan and dust with cornmeal. Roll out pizza dough (or toss n pull if you must) on a floured board with a little cornmeal and pop it on there. Array top with cheez, olives, sliced sausages, and beet rounds. Sprinkle with a little salt and pepper, olive oil, italian herbs. Brush the edge of the pizza with a little olive oil and sprinkle with garlic powder.

Bake for 18-20 minutes or until done to your liking.

Prefer to make your own sausages? I would go with ⅓ mushroom flour, ⅓ almond flour, and ⅓ half each tapioca starch and potato starch… mix in tomato paste, smoked salt, sage, chili flakes, garlic, onion powder, and a little mustard. Clearly you should shape them like little baseball bats. Give them a steam or nuke. Or do you know how to oven smoke? Soak some wood chips in water, drain, and place in the bottom of a broiling pan. Set the grate over the top as you normally would (a broiling pan typically has one of these, if not someone lost it!) and place your "sausages" atop. Make a dome of foil over the top and seal it tightly.

Make sure the foil is sealed tight, if the smoke leaks out too much you may really have a fun time with the neighbors. What can you do with a little smoke? It's such a joke but what can you lose?

250 degrees for 4 to 6 hours. Aren't you sorry you asked now?

HAVANA PIZZA AFFAIR
PIZZA FOR ALL
BABY BABY MAKE ME LOCO BABY BABY MAKE ME MAM
PIZZA FOR ME

★HAVANA PIZZA AFFAIR

1 C. cubanelle peppers, seeded and sliced

½ C. mango, peeled and diced

1 plantain, peeled and sliced into ¼" thick rounds

½ C. cooked black beans, seasoned

1 C. vegan chickn, chopped and sauteed with paprika, salt and pepper

2 Tbsp. cilantro, chopped

1 C. onion, diced

For the Mojo

Blend:

⅔ C. orange juice

1 Tbsp. lime juice

3-4 peeled, smashed garlic cloves

2-3 Tbsp. olive oil

Salt & pepper

1 Tbsp. chopped fresh oregano

1 tsp. Cumin

Add 1 Tbsp. tomato paste to thicken a bit and then mix with the marinara

1 C. marinara (see Go Little Marinara pg. 65)

1 C. grated cheez or cheez sauce
Pizza dough for 1 pizza

Hey I was thinkin' of havin' a affair myself! Don't tell me it's "an affair," we're not going to argue with the boys from Queens unless you want to be haunted mercilessly, anyway...

You're going to have to do something to these black beans, plain ones on a pizza? Now that's just gross. This is one of the uses of extra mojo...baby baby make me mango.

Prepare pizza dough and into the pan it goes. The pizza pan, that is.

Now, like pick a banana...

Slice plantain, fry on each side 2-3 minutes, now take them in a single layer and flatten the buggers, dip in water, pat dry with paper towels, and then fry again, don't splash yourself, fry for another minute or two until crispy. Toss with salt and pepper and set on a paper towel somewhere. If that all seems familiar it's because they are tostones. I learnt it when I was sent to spy on a Cuban talent show.

You can cut up the fried plantains or leave them as they are, perhaps a big bit on a pizza slice.

Spread most of the sauce on the pizza. Toss the beans and chickn with the rest. Array the chickn, herbs, and vegetables atop and then the cheez. Bake at 450 degrees for 15 minutes, take it out and put the fried plantain on top and bake for another 5 minutes. Garnish with fresh cilantro, hooray for the USA!

People who don't like fruit on pizza may drop dead from witnessing this. It's like Castro's exploding conch mind-blowing.

Hope you got that PT boat ready because I am outta here.

★EVERY TIME I EAT VEGETABLES IT MAKES ME THINK OF YOU

For the Vegetable Crust

2 C. grated potato

½ C. roasted cauliflower

½ C. grated carrot

½ C. cassava flour

½ C. farina (instead of farina, use corn meal, flax meal or millet flour for gluten free)

¼ C. olive oil

salt, pepper

1 C. halved cherry tomatoes

½ C. thinly sliced red onion, oregano

Olive oil

2 C. separated broccolini, sauteed

1 C. chopped cauliflower, roasted with 1 tsp. curry powder and 1 Tbsp. lemon juice

1 ½ C. pizza sauce (see EXTRA! recipe pg. 24)

¼ C. pine nuts

Tahini cheez or favorite cheez (for tahini, see Shreddable Cheez recipe pg. 18)

Thorazine (optional)

Yes I know some of these are tubers… so are you! Trust me, any of these will make a true veg-hater gag.

This time mix the crust ingredients together and place in a greased, deep 14-16" pan or you can use an 8x14 casserole dish for this ow-ooooow. Press him in there gently and avoid a bad affair, and pre-bake for 15 minutes at 400 degrees. Next put the sauce on there, then the cheez and then the remaining vegetables and sprinkle with pine nuts. Bake at 350 degrees for 25-30 minutes. You'll have to serve this bugger like a casserole. It would be good to make some more white or red sauce and heat it up and serve with that. Some of that hemp parm would be good on there also (see Hey Ho Let's Pizza Dough pg. 12).

Speaking of gags, you can leave out the farina in the crust for wheat free, and you can probably leave out the thorazine or equivalent unless you're on it already, no judging although you will turn into a head of lettuce.

Give serious consideration to laying parchment down under this fiasco before baking.

★PIZZAMAN

1 lb. or so cooked french fries (yes included my own french fry recipe on pg. 87) If you want to make your own french fries, you will need a little more than a lb. of potatoes, salt & pepper, and oil to fry.

Salt and pepper

6 garlic cloves, peeled and smashed

¼ C. olive oil

2 Tbsp. chopped parsley

1 Tbsp. white wine vinegar

Pizza sauce (see EXTRA! recipe pg. 24)

Pizza dough for 1 pizza

2 Tbsp. of your favorite mayonnaise

1 C. grated "mozzarella" (in this rare case I would combine with an amusing yellow cheez as well, feel free to use more cheez if there's one you love)... or use one of the other cheezy sauces in this book, or pesto

Optional: caramelized onions and minced pickles for "animal style"

I went to a pizza place once in Massa Lubrense and they had one called "Spidey" that had french fries on it… they were mortified when I ordered it and tried to talk me out of it, to no avail. It was great! After that for a while I put french fries on my pizza all the time. Also the place was full of cops and because it was Italy that means about 8 different types of cops since they have all sorts. Pizza is probably like donuts to them. If the boys from Queens sang about cops more, there would probably be a donut pizza on here somewhere.

Prepare the pizza dough and get it in a liberally greased pan. Preheat oven to 450 degrees.

Mix together pizza sauce and mayonnaise… if you want to get daring, use a vegan tartar sauce. I'm not going to add ketchup to this, that is a step too far but it is getting slightly into "special sauce" territory nonetheless. Think this is gross? Listen bud, don't be a radioactive butt.

Blend garlic, parsley, vinegar, olive oil, and a little salt until smooth. Add a little broth if necessary. Set aside.

Spread sauce over this, followed by cheez. Next array the french fries, then drizzle or dab with the garlic mixture.

Bake for about 20 minutes or until it seems done to your liking.

If you can fold the slice up, really it's like putting french fries on a falafel sandwich or a po' boy at that point, so all good.

Secrets to good french fries include an ice water bath and double frying, with the second fry at a higher temperature. I mean, do you want to cook or not?

Peel the potatoes and cut into ½" sticks, a little thinner is fine too if you like that better. Place in a bowl of cold water as you do this. Let them sit in there for about half an hour, then drain and pat dry with paper towels on a baking sheet.

Heat oil in a deep pot to 300 degrees and fry the potatoes in batches for around 3-4 minutes, don't let them brown at this point. Next drain them and place on absorbent paper to get rid of some of the grease. Raise the temp to 350-400 degrees (in that range is fine), and fry them again this time until browned to your liking. Drain again and shake with salt and pepper.

Put it on the pi-zzaaaaa!

★SHEENA IS A CRUST LOVER

Pizza dough for 1 pizza

1 ¾ C. marinara (see Go Little Marinara pg. 65)

2 Tbsp. tomato paste

¼ C. orange juice

1 tsp. dried oregano

12 asparagus spears cut into thirds

1 tomato, very thinly sliced

1 C. red onion, sliced thinly

1 Tbsp. olive oil

½ C. thinly sliced pepperoncini

Salt and pepper

Parm sprinkle or "wheat germ" (see Hey Ho Let's Pizza Dough pg. 9 or Imitation Wheat Germ recipe pg. 25)

For those that love their dough-oh-oh, you'll like this style. Prepare the dough as you would but this time use a 12" pan. Roll out the dough on a floured board to fit your pizza pan and set it in there. Allow to rise for 1 hour. At the end of this time, use your hands to push the middle of the dough down and the edge up, you'll want to ensure that the dough doesn't blart over the edge of the pan, keep it tidy. If you're dirty they won't let you into the discotheque-a-go-go.

Mix marinara sauce, tomato paste, and orange juice together and spread over the dough.

Heat oven to 450 degrees.

Heat olive oil in a pan and saute asparagus and red onion with salt and pepper and oregano. Once the onions are translucent, it's ready.

Array slices of tomato on your pizza punk-punk, then asparagus and onion (careful not to burn yourself). Next the pepperoncini.

Bake for 15 minutes, take it out and sprinkle with the parm and then bake for another 10 minutes. Should be ready!

If you want the dough a bit more biscuit-y, add a teaspoon of baking powder to the dough recipe, all the more dough-y for your doughy times, you can really have it all!

What might make this pizza more punk-punk, since it doesn't seem very punk-punk, you ask?...wheat germ, wheat germ is the only thing that would work.

I HAD ENOUGH OF THAT CRUMMY STUFFED CRUST.
MMMMM CRUMMY STUFF

★WELL I'M AGAINST IT

It's a Pineapple Pizza...

1 pineapple, peeled and cored, sliced into 12 rings

½ tsp. to 1 tsp. smoked paprika

Several Tbsp. olive oil to use variously

1 C. veggie ham, chopped

Pizza dough for 1 pizza

2 C. pizza sauce (see EXTRA! recipe pg. 24)

½ C. diced onion

12 baby red onions, peeled

2 C. beet juice

¼ C. red wine vinegar

Salt and pepper

Bay leaf

½ tsp. coriander seeds

1 C. grated cheez

Come on come on it ain't so bad. Although I, too, do not like fun for anyone.

Lightly coat pineapple rings with olive oil and lime juice. Add a little salt, pepper, and smoked paprika to the pineapple rings.

Place the pineapple rings on a lightly greased baking pan in a single layer and broil, turning once, for probably 5-7 minutes per side until it looks pretty good.

People associate pineapple rings with cherries, I have a more fun idea... pickled baby onions! Bring beet juice, red wine vinegar, salt & pepper, bay leaf, and coriander seeds to a boil then lower to a simmer for a few minutes, add peeled onions and simmer for 5-7 minutes. Then place a lid on top and turn off heat. Allow to sit until cooled then put them in the fridge overnight, remove bay leaf before use.

Prepare pizza dough as usual and place on the ol' greased pan. Heat oven to 450 degrees.

Slather pizza dough with sauce, then sprinkle with chopped ham and onions. Then add the cheez. Next, array the pineapple slices attractively and place a pickled baby onion in the middle of each.

Bake 18-25 minutes or until done to your liking (seriously yes, the baking time on this one can vary wildly, for a lot of reasons).

★MAKIN' MONSTER SLICES

2 C. baby arugula

Pizza dough (if you're using a larger pizza pan, it would be very thin crust to just use 1 crust's worth of dough, which is great and all, however feel free to increase recipe by ⅓ the amount or ½ if you don't like a super thin crust)

2 ½ C. pizza sauce (see EXTRA! recipe pg. 24)

1 ½ C. grated cheez

Salt and pepper

Couple Tbsp. olive oil

Chili flakes

1 can of off-brand circular spaghetti hoops

The easiest way to do a monster slice is just to use the largest pizza pan you have (like 16" or 18") and then cut it into only four slices at the end, and there you go. If you fuck it up I'll call 254 so they won't blame me.

Prepare the pizza dough as always and get it in the greased pan of your choice.

Slather with pizza sauce and sprinkle cheez on. Open spaghetti hoops, open can of worms, and dump those on there. Every day's a holiday.

Bake at 450 degrees for 18-20 minutes.

When it's done, throw the arugula over the top and sprinkle with salt, pepper, and a drizzle of Olive oil, bedazzle with chili flakes, cut and serve.

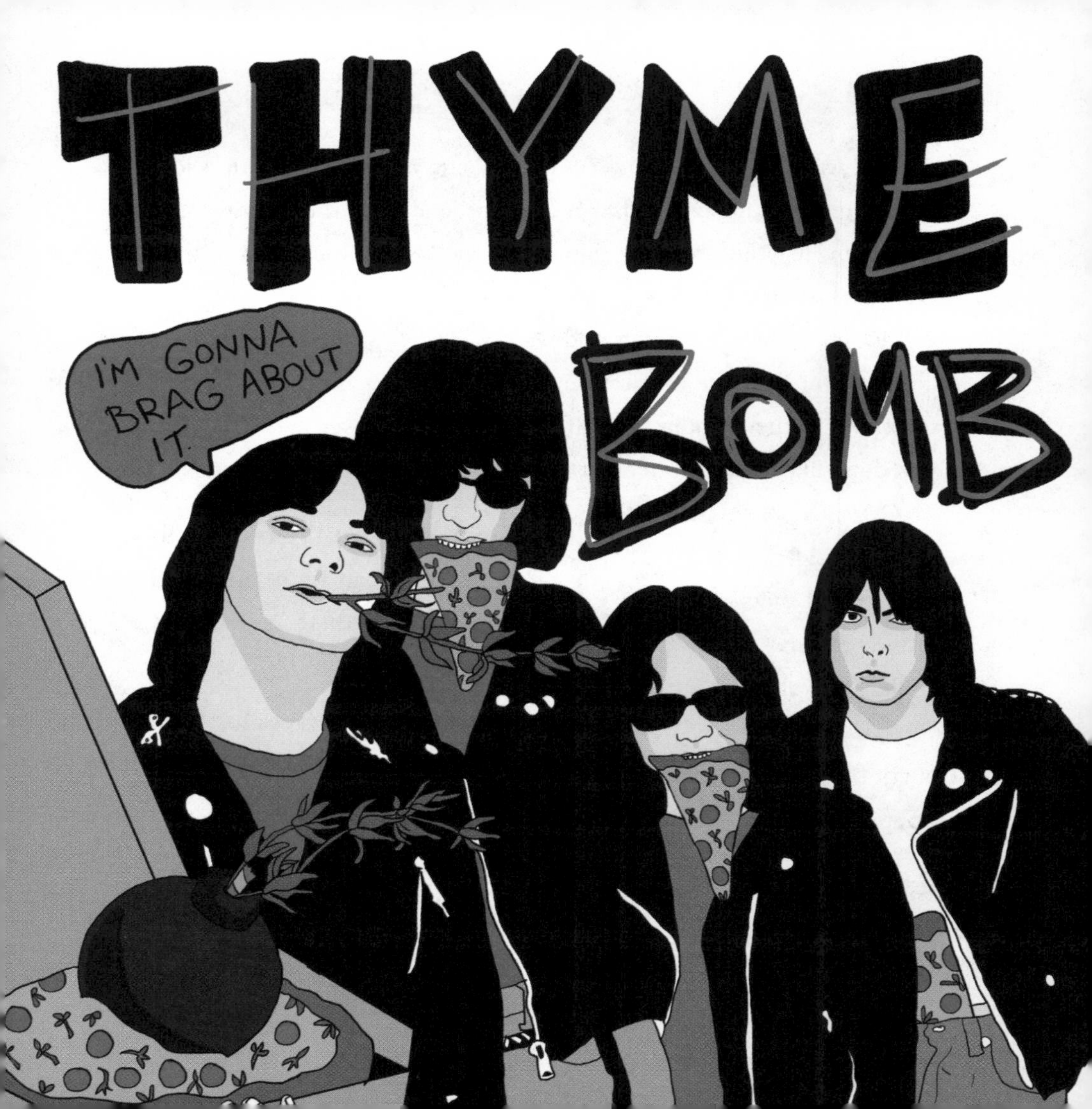
THYME
BOMB
I'M GONNA BRAG ABOUT IT.

★THYME BOMB

Pizza dough for 1 pizza

2 C. pizza sauce (see EXTRA! recipe pg. 24)

1 C. cheez, grated

½ tsp. dried thyme

2 Tbsp. fresh thyme leaves

½ C. chopped Italian parsley

¼ C. olive oil

1 Tbsp. lemon juice

1 Tbsp. red wine vinegar

1 C. coarsely chopped white onion

4 cloves garlic, peeled and smashed

1 serrano chili, seeded and coarsely chopped

Salt

So good, you're gonna brag about it!

Doing basically a chimichurri-style sauce with thyme for this one, a familiar taste made a little harsher. Kill your parents-harsh? Yeah maybe. Drop outta school!

In a food processor, chop thyme leaves, parsley, onion, garlic, chili, vinegar, and lemon juice with salt to taste, slowly add oil until it looks pretty good. Set aside or put it in the fridge to flavor up.

Prepare the pizza dough like we told you before. Preheat oven to 450 degrees. Slather pizza sauce on dough and sprinkle with dried thyme. If you want to put on any toppings, do that next. Then the thyme sauce, dollop that around the pizza. And at last the cheez.

Bake for 20 minutes, less or more depending on how done it's lookin'.

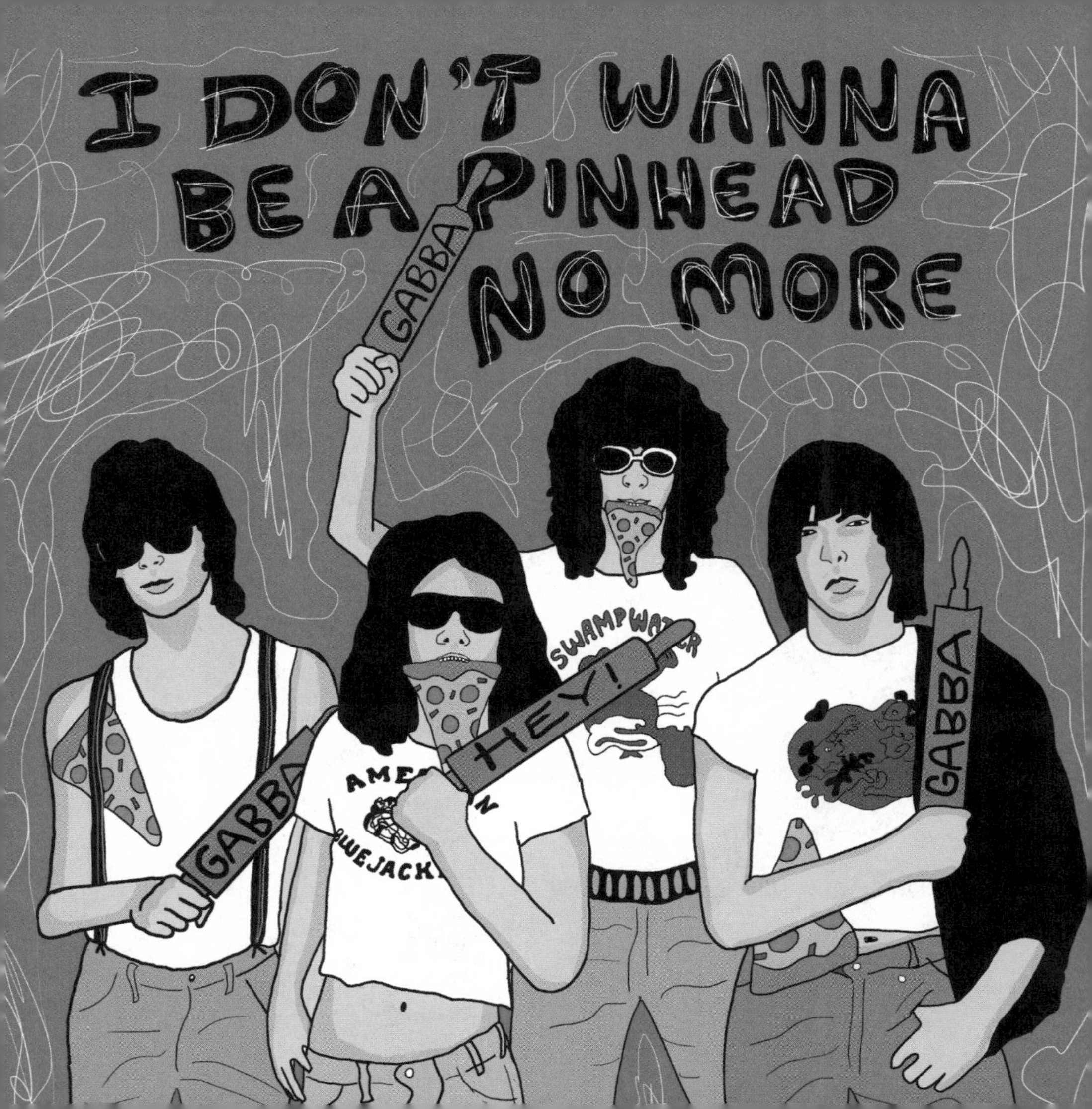
I DON'T WANNA BE A PINHEAD NO MORE
GABBA
GABBA
HEY!
GABBA

★PINHEAD

1 ¾ C. pizza sauce w/ 1 ½ tsp. curry powder added and ¼ C. orange juice (see EXTRA! recipe pg. 24)

Pizza dough for 1 pizza

2 sheets roasted seaweed (sushi nori), cut into thin strips

2 C. peeled cubed taro root or extra firm tofu

A little umeboshi vinegar

Couple Tbsp. tamari or liquid aminos

1 C. corn

1 C. diced onion

1 C. grated cheez or cheez sauce, use an exciting, spicy flavor

Couple Tbsp. olive oil

2 Tbsp. chopped cilantro

2 Tbsp. chopped thai basil

Prepare pizza dough and get it in the pan. Marinate taro or tofu in plum vinegar, tamari, and salt and pepper to taste. Meanwhile coat corn with a little oil, salt and pepper, and broil that for about 5-6 minutes gabba-gabba hey. Set aside.

Fry taro or tofu in olive oil for a couple of minutes, add onion… when it starts to brown that's good enough, one of us. Set aside and mix with seaweed strips.

Slather pizza with sauce. Next the corn and cheez and then array the taro, onion, and seaweed atop this and bake at 450 degrees for 18-20 minutes. Sprinkle with cilantro and thai basil.

So much good for your brain in this recipe, eat this pizza and it will make you S-M-A-R-T.

★GLAD TO SEE YOU GO (in my mouth)

1 bunch chopped spinach

1 C. sliced mushroom

2 minced garlic cloves

½ c. diced onion

2 Tbsp. olive oil

1 C. kreem cheez

Pizza dough for 1 pizza

1 C. pizza sauce or white sauce, more if you like (see EXTRA! recipe pg.
   24 or Here Today… pg. 110)

1 C. grated cheez

For the Mac Uncheez

2 C. cooked penne or macaroni

1/4 C. sauerkraut

1/3 C. cashews

 2 Tbsp. miso

1 Tbsp. prepared mustard, salt, and white pepper to taste

1/4 C. diced onion

2 Tbsp. lemon juice (or more)

a splash of white balsamic or red wine vinegar

1/2 to 1 C. mushroom broth (more or less depending on thickness you
   want)

1/4 C. tahini

2 or 3 garlic cloves

2 Tbsp. tapioca or potato starch (use more if needed)

Blend it together, season to taste. Cook over low heat, stirring until it thickens up a bit. Mix in cooked pasta. Finish by seasoning to taste.

Prepare that ol' pizza dough and get it in the pan. Saute mushrooms, onion, spinach, and garlic in olive oil with a little salt and pepper.

Spread kreem cheez over pizza dough, then white or pizza sauce, then sauteed veg. Now evenly do the mac uncheez on there, now the cheez (always room for more haha!).

Bake at 425 degrees for 20-25 minutes and in a moment of passion get the glory like Charles Manson. He was mostly known for his pizzas.

★COME BACK, BABY

Eggplant, cut into 12 ½" rounds and sprinkled with salt

½ C. cornmeal

½ C. rice flour

1 C. soda water

Salt and pepper

½ C. red onion, thinly sliced

2 bulbs garlic, and a little oil and salt to apply to these

12-24 basil leaves

6 slices vegan cheez (white), cut in half

2 C. pizza sauce (see EXTRA! recipe pg. 24)

Pizza dough for 1 pizza

1 C. grated cheez

Oil to fry

For the Parm Mixture

1 C. ground hemp seeds

¼ C. nutritional yeast

1 tsp. Salt

1 tsp. lemon pepper

½ tsp. garlic powder

Cut tops off garlic bulbs, slather with oil, sprinkle with salt and wrap in foil, leaving the tops exposed. Then bake at 400 degrees for 25 minutes, cool, peel, and separate cloves. Set aside.

Saute eggplant in hot oil for 2-3 minutes. Remove from heat. Coat in parm mixture and fry again, turning once, until browned. Drain and cool a bit. Eggplant "parm" is great, I found out how to make it a little too late oh yes I did now. Mix corn meal, rice flour, soda water, and salt and pepper to taste. You might need to use a bit more liquid, it should be the consistency of pancake batter or a little thinner. Set aside in a large bowl. Place a piece of cheez on each slice of eggplant and dredge in cornmeal batter, and fry again, turning once and taking care not to let the cheez slide off.

Prepare pizza dough in pan, slather with pizza sauce, place onion and eggplant slices, then sprinkle with more of the parm mixture and grated cheez. Array with basil leaves. Bake at 450 degrees for 20 minutes.

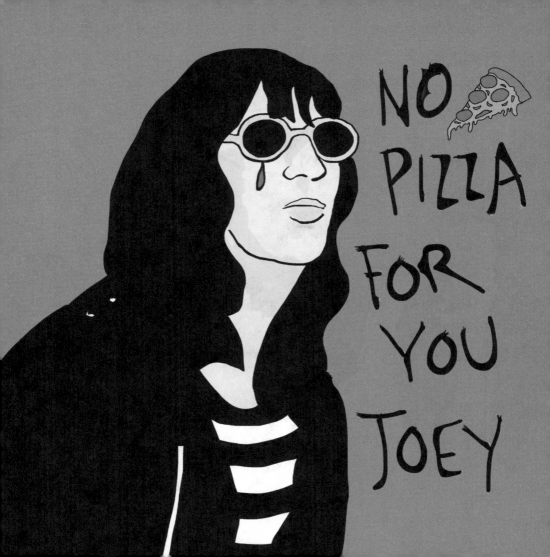

★HERE TODAY GONE TOMORROW

Pizza dough for 1 pizza

1 C. grated white cheez

1/2 C. sliced shiitakes

1 C. separated oyster mushrooms

½ C. halved crimini

½ C. chopped maitake or matsutake

½ C. thinly sliced white onion

2 cloves garlic, peeled and thinly sliced

Salt and pepper to taste

For the White Sauce

¼ C. olive oil

¼ C. flour

1 Tbsp. white wine vinegar

½ C. mushroom broth

¾ C. kreemer

1 tsp. dried Italian herbs

½ tsp. white pepper

2 cloves garlic, peeled & crushed

1 tsp. onion powder

2 Tbsp. truffle oil

This one is great, I tell you I just can't take it, you'll have to make it… or else you'll never have thaaat recipeee agaaaain… ohhh noooo!

Prepare pizza dough as usual and get it in the pan. Preheat oven to 450 degrees.

To make a white sauce, blend 2 Tbsp. olive oil, flour, broth, 1 Tbsp. truffle oil, salt, crushed garlic, onion powder, vinegar, herbs, and kreem together. Heat in a saucepan til it bubbles and thickens a bit, stirring occasionally. Add white pepper and season to taste. Allow to sit and cool off a bit.

One nice variation of this would be to add a little prepared horseradish after the sauce is cooked, just stir in a tablespoon, adds some kick.

Saute mushrooms, onions, and sliced garlic in 2 Tbsp. olive oil just for a couple of minutes, until they sweat a bit.

Slather pizza crust with white sauce, sprinkle cheez on, then decorate with mushrooms and onions. Bake for 20 minutes or so.

Take it out of the oven and drizzle with the rest of the truffle oil, you can also sprinkle with truffle salt if you're feeling bougie.

★GIMME GIMME SHOCK TREATMENT

1 C. crushed tortilla chips

2 Tbsp. chili sauce

2 C. pizza sauce (see EXTRA! recipe pg. 24)

1 Tbsp. chili powder

2 diced jalapenos

1 C. diced white onion

2 minced garlic cloves

½ C. tomatillos

1 C. vegan egg or tofu scramble

A dozen strips pickled nopalitos

½ C. soy chorizo or make your own with another legume

A couple Tbsp. olive oil

Salt and pepper

1 C. grated cheez

Pizza dough for 1 pizza

Lime

Sour kreem

Prepare your pizza dough and git it in the pan.

Don't feel sick or lose your mind, I figure chilaquiles or some resemblance would be fairly shocking on a pizza unless you've had it before. Technically this is chilaquiles con "huevos."

Saute tortilla chips, soy chorizo, onion, garlic, tomatillos, jalapenos in olive oil and add a little salt and pepper and chili powder. After a few minutes add ½ C. pizza sauce and chili sauce. Continue cooking until this mixture starts to brown in places. Add "egg" or tofu and mix. Set aside.

Slather pizza with pizza sauce, array with tortilla chip mixture, then grated cheez, then decorate with cactus strips. Bake at 450 degrees for about 20 minutes.

Serve with sour kreem and lime, and some fresh tortilla chips crushed on top. Now you can wake up and face the day!

Side of salsa wouldn't hurt.

★I WANTED EVERYTHING (on my pizza)

Pizza dough for 1 pizza

2 C. half pizza sauce and half marinara (or other combo see EXTRA! recipe pg. 24 and Go Little Marinara pg. 65)

1 C. cashew cheez sauce (see Now I Wanna Sniff Cashews pg. 15)

1 C. grated cheez

½ C. sauteed broccoli

½ C. diced onion

½ C. sliced olives

12-24 small pieces veggie sausage

12-24 slices veggie pepperoni

12 basil leaves

12 cherry tomatoes, halved

½ C. julienne sundried tomatoes

½ C. diced red bell peppers

Sorry, no pineapple. If you thought there would be, it was dreaming and fantasy!

For this of course you want to prepare the pizza dough as usual and get it in a greased pan. Slather with the pizza sauce-marinara mix. Sprinkle with half the toppings, then the cheez, then the other half of the toppings and drizzle with cashew sauce.

Bake at 450 degreees for about 22 minutes and think about how you've had the world on your shoulders since you've gotten older.

This pizza has just about everything, but feel free to add everything else you can think of.

★CHASING THE NIGHT PIZZA

For the Tapenade

2 C. chopped olives

¼ C. minced red bell pepper

¼ C. minced red onion

2 Tbsp. chopped parsley

¼ C. chopped basil

2 Tbsp. capers

1 Tbsp. balsamic vinegar

2-3 minced garlic cloves

2-3 Tbsp. olive oil

Salt and pepper

Pizza dough for 1 pizza

1 ½ C. pizza sauce or marinara (see EXTRA! recipe pg. 24 or Go Little Marinara Go pg. 65)

1-2 tsp. charcoal powder

1 C. scary looking cheez or 1 C. grated tahini cheez using black sesame instead of regular (see Shreddable Cheez recipe with tahini variation pg. 18)

Prepare pizza dough as you would except add 1-2 tsp. charcoal powder. Get it in the pan.

Feelin' hot yeah you're on fiyaaaahhh!

Make your tapenade. Mix the ingredients for it together in a bowl and season to taste. Put in refrigerator, covered, until ready to use.

Spread sauce on pizza, then most of the tapenade. Sprinkle on cheez, then dollop the rest of the tapenade, however you like, live your life as you choose. It's intoxicating. Bake at 450 degrees for 18-20 minutes.

Fun additions: black garlic

★KKK TOOK MY LAST SLICE AWAY

This is a waffle pizza, alternatively you could do it on a mound of crackers

1 C. hash browns, cooked to perfection and separated

½ C. chopped onion

½ C. chopped tomato

1 C. cooked vegan egg or tofu scramble

½ C. chopped veggie sausage

½ C. chopped veggie bacon, sauteed

1 C. grated cheez or cheez sauce

1 C. pizza sauce w/ 1 Tbsp. ketchup added

For the Gravy

2 Tbsp. flour, 1 C. broth, ½ C. soy or cashew milk, 2 Tbsp. tamari, salt and pepper to taste, 1 tsp onion powder, 1 tsp, garlic powder, ½ C. chopped mushrooms, ½ tsp. dried fines herbes, ½ C. diced onion, 2-3 Tbsp. oil or margarine

There are two ways to do this gravy, you can toast flour in a pan until lightly browned (1-2 minutes), whisk in the oil to make a paste, cook for about one minute, then whisk in the liquid thoroughly and add everything else and simmer for 5-10 minutes. The other way is easier, just whisk flour into milk and broth then add everything else and simmer for 5-10 minutes.

For the Waffle

Mix 2 C. flour, 2 tsp. baking powder, 1 pkg. yeast, 1 Tbsp. nutritional yeast, 1 Tbsp. sugar, ½ tsp. garlic powder, 1 tsp. dried italian herbs, 1 tsp. salt, 1 ⅓ C. unsweetened vegan milk

Allow to stand for 30 minutes in a warm place, and preheat your waffle maker if you want the first one to get done right or else it'll never get there, it'll never get there, it'll never get there they say, then make a couple of large waffles.

For some reason the KKK reminds me of waffles, I mean sorry waffles, no offense it just seems like something they would like. So let's make waffles! In order for this to be more pizza-y, we'll make this a yeast dough which is a little weird.

Really if this is the theme, the sauce should probably be mayonnaise (but not too spicy!).

For an even better version, replace half the batter with mac uncheez.

So what you're going to want to do is heat the oven to 425 degrees, then set the waffles on a greased pan, hopefully covering the whole thing with waffle. This is messy so a large casserole is probably a good idea. Next spread pizza sauce on, followed by half of the gravy. Next the toppings (except the potatoes), next the cheez and then the potatoes. Bake for 15-20 minutes or until the cheez looks pretty good. Serve with the rest of the gravy.

Also good to top with sauteed onions and mushrooms, more chopped tomatoes and more cheez. Ring up the president!

★ WALL OF PIZZA

Pizza dough, full amount from recipe

3 C. marinara (see Go Little Marinara pg. 65)

2 C. grated cheez or cheez sauce

2 C. sauteed broccolini with a little salt and pepper

1 ½ C. kreem cheez or crumbled seasoned tofu or mashed seasoned garbanzo beans, add a little lemon juice, salt, olive oil, and garlic powder regardless

2 minced garlic cloves

1 C. chopped onion

1 Tbsp. minced fresh herbs

1 C. chopped olives

1 C. chopped roasted red bell peppers

For this you're going to need a rather large casserole dish that is pretty deep. Divide the pizza dough into four balls and roll each out on a floured board to fit your pan size, whatever it is. You should then griddle or fry each one, turning once, for only a minute or two per side. You could also pre-bake at 400 degrees for 5 minutes. You'll see why in a minute here.

Mix the vegetables, herbs, garlic, and olives together and set aside.

Grease your casserole, coat the bottom of the pan with some marinara. Lay down a pizza dough, then ⅓ of kreem cheez, ⅓ of vegetables, and ¼ of the sauce, followed by ¼ of cheez. Repeat this process for the next two layers. At the end you of course put the last pizza dough on top and you should have only a bit of marinara and cheez remaining, which you will spread on the top. Bake at 375 degrees with foil on top for 25 minutes, then remove the foil and bake it for another 10-15 minutes. All set! Don't imprison or shoot anyone!

★I CAN'T GIVE YOU ANYTHING ON YOUR PIZZA

Pizza dough, you've got the recipe

Oil to fry

Seasoning salt

Form dough into a ball and grease lightly, place in a bowl and cover with a cloth and allow to rise for a couple of hours.

Preheat oil in a deep pan to 350 degrees. Divide the dough into 4 balls and roll out 4 pizza crusts from this on a floured board. About ¼" thick is fine. Fry these one at a time in the oil until browned and drain on absorbent paper. Sprinkle with seasoned salt and serve with a nice sauce such as marinara, pesto, white, fry sauce…make up your mind! All in this book, friends! Yes, I am kinda cute.

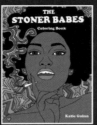

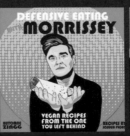

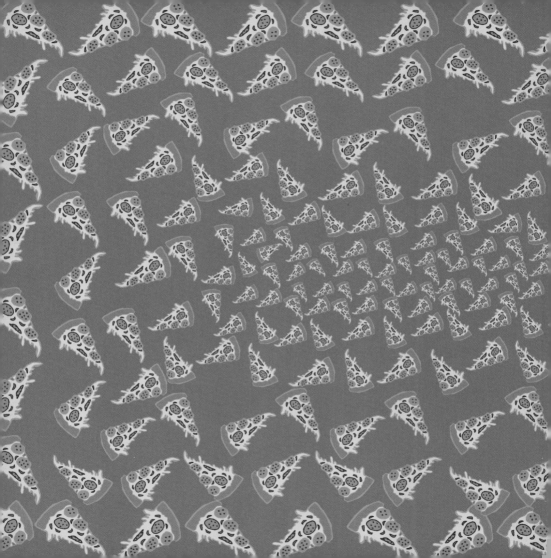